KITTEN LADY'S CATIVITY BOOK

This book belongs to:

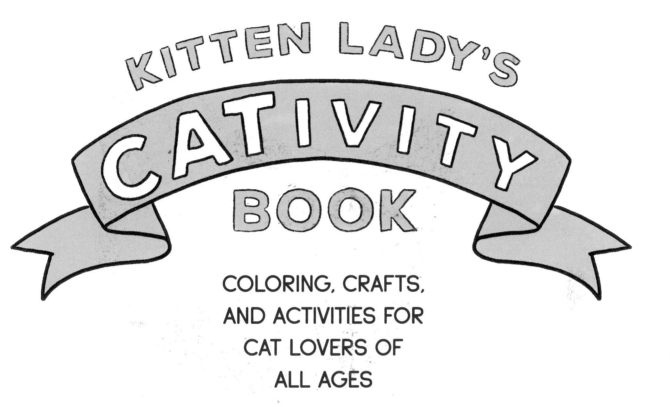

KITTEN LADY'S CATIVITY BOOK

COLORING, CRAFTS,
AND ACTIVITIES FOR
CAT LOVERS OF
ALL AGES

HANNAH SHAW & MEGAN LYNN KOTT

HARVEST
An Imprint of WILLIAM MORROW

HarperCollins books may be purchased for educational, business, or sales promotional use.
For information, please email the Special Markets Department at SPsales@harpercollins.com.
FIRST EDITION
Designed by Stephanie Hays
Illustrated by Megan Lynn Kott
Library of Congress Cataloging-in-Publication Data has been applied for.
ISBN 978-0-358-72453-7
22 23 24 25 26 RTL 10 9 8 7 6 5 4 3 2 1

TABLE OF CONTENTS

MEET HANNAH AND MEGAN

...and their cats!

HANNAH   MEGAN

COCO

ELOISE

DAVOS

AURORA

HAROUN

FERGUSON

GRIFFIN

THESSALY

WELCOME TO
THE CATIVITY BOOK

I'm Hannah, also known as Kitten Lady! I'm a professional kitten rescuer and humane educator. These are my cats, Coco, Eloise, Haroun, and Ferguson!

And I'm Megan! I'm a professional artist specializing in cats. These are my cats, Davos, Aurora, Griffin, and Thessaly!

We're passionate animal advocates and good friends, and we're here to welcome you into the wonderful world of feline welfare! If you're as much of a cat lover as we are, you know that love isn't just a feeling you have for cats, but an action you take on their behalf. And what better way to practice taking action than through fun, informative, and compassion-building activities?

Now it's time to grab your favorite colored pencils, crayons, or water-based markers and bring this book to life! The pages that follow are packed with adorable drawings for you to color and educational activities to enjoy both on and off the page. We hope you love coloring, puzzling, and crafting with us, but even more than that—we hope you feel inspired to do more to make the world a better place for cats!

xo,
Hannah and Megan

GETTING TO KNOW CATS

Every cat is a unique individual with their own physical characteristics, personality traits, and preferences. One of the many joys of adopting a feline friend is getting to know who they are and what makes them purr! Whether you're admiring their coat pattern, figuring out their favorite place to be scratched, or contemplating their complex inner life, it's a magical experience to discover what makes each cat so wonderfully special.

In this section, you'll do activities that help you get to know and love cats—inside and out!

DECODING YOUR CAT'S SECRET NAME

So you've named your cat Sprinkles or Bella or Max. Those are great names, but did you know that every cat has a secret name that only they know? It's true! All cats have an internal life and language of their own, and while it was long thought that no one could crack the code and discover the secret names of cats, we've unearthed an ancient decoding system that does just that. You may call your cat "Oreo," but look at the secret name decoder below and you'll soon find that your cat's true name is...

THE AMAZING DOODLE BEANS!

Instructions: Find the words that correspond with the first 3 letters of your cat's name.

	First letter	Second letter	Third letter
A	Professor	Fluffy	Flufflepuff
B	Mr./Mrs.	Baby	Patootie
C	Sir/Madam	Cutie	Boo Boo
D	Super	Furry	Claw
E	Sweet	Squeaky	Beans
F	Li'l	Taco	Cuddlesworth
G	Tiny	Lumpy	Poops-A-Lot
H	Big	Brave	Pants
I	President	Hissy	Fluffkins
J	Mighty	Fancy	McGee
K	Captain	Stinky	McGillicutty
L	General	Poopy	Face
M	Lord/Lady	Candy	Panther
N	Special Agent	Chunky	Softy
O	The Amazing	Itty-Bitty	Meowzers
P	Baby	Mini	Peabody
Q	King/Queen	Silly	Catsby
R	Duke/Duchess	Doodle	Fang
S	Doctor	Sneaky	Booty
T	The Magnificent	Wonder	Snoot
U	Señor/Señora	Sassy	Belly
V	Officer	Chester	von Hunter
W	DJ	Spicy	Purrington
X	Prince/Princess	Pizza	Hiss-A-Lot
Y	Grandpa/Grandma	Puppy	Bear
Z	Ultra	Cranky	Paw

Your cat's name:

Your cat's secret name:

Your cat's name:

Your cat's secret name:

Your cat's name:

Your cat's secret name:

Your cat's name:

Your cat's secret name:

5

MY BEST FELINE FRIEND

Fill in the blanks with special information about your cat companions!

_____ is a _____ cat with _____ ,
(NAME)   (COLOR)   (SPECIAL FEATURE)

_____ , and _____ .
(SPECIAL FEATURE)   (SPECIAL FEATURE)

Their favorite activities are _____ and _____ .
(ACTIVITY)   (ACTIVITY)

Their favorite possessions are their _____ ,
(ITEM)

their _____ , and their _____ .
(ITEM)   (ITEM)

I'll never forget the day I met them, when _____
(ORIGIN STORY)

_____
(ORIGIN STORY CONTINUED)

_____ !
(ORIGIN STORY CONTINUED)

Now we're good friends, and we love to _____ !
(SHARED ACTIVITY)

Color your cat here!

_____ is a _____ cat with _____ ,
(NAME)   (COLOR)   (SPECIAL FEATURE)

_____ , and _____ .
(SPECIAL FEATURE)   (SPECIAL FEATURE)

Their favorite activities are _____ and _____ .
                                    (ACTIVITY)   (ACTIVITY)

Their favorite possessions are their _____ ,
                                            (ITEM)

their _____ , and their _____ .
           (ITEM)   (ITEM)

I'll never forget the day I met them, when _____
                                                  (ORIGIN STORY)

_____
(ORIGIN STORY CONTINUED)

_____ !
(ORIGIN STORY CONTINUED)

Now we're good friends, and we love to _____ !
                                              (SHARED ACTIVITY)

_____ is a _____ cat with _____ ,
(NAME)   (COLOR)   (SPECIAL FEATURE)

_____ , and _____ .
(SPECIAL FEATURE)   (SPECIAL FEATURE)

Their favorite activities are _____ and _____ .
                                    (ACTIVITY)   (ACTIVITY)

Their favorite possessions are their _____ ,
                                            (ITEM)

their _____ , and their _____ .
           (ITEM)   (ITEM)

I'll never forget the day I met them, when _____
                                                  (ORIGIN STORY)

_____
(ORIGIN STORY CONTINUED)

_____ !
(ORIGIN STORY CONTINUED)

Now we're good friends, and we love to _____ !
                                              (SHARED ACTIVITY)

WHAT'S YOUR CAT'S PURRSONALITY TYPE?

How does your cat greet you when you come home?

A. Meeting you at the door, meowing.

B. Looking at you briefly to acknowledge your existence. Or not.

C. Jumping into your arms, purring and drooling.

D. Untying your shoelaces for you.

E. Hiding under the porch until the coast is clear.

How does your cat prefer to dine?

A. Begging you for treats nonstop.

B. Taking their time eating solo.

C. Sitting at the dinner table with you.

D. Breaking into the kibble when no one's looking.

E. Sneaking into the trash can.

What's your cat's favorite toy?

A. A high-flying feather wand.

B. Their own pesky tail.

C. Your hair or beard.

D. Literally anything—crumpled-up receipts, socks, light reflected on a wall.

E. A squirmy bug.

Where does your cat sleep at night?

A. At the foot of your bed.

B. Perched on top of a cat tree, alone.

C. On top of your head.

D. Sleep? What's sleep?!

E. They're a night owl and are usually out and about.

Your cat is looking out the window. What are they thinking?

A. "I hope that person is coming to pet me!"

B. "Isn't it amazing to imagine how many butterflies are flapping their wings at the very same time...whoa..."

C. "This blanket sure is squishy."

D. "Hey, squirrel! I *dare* you to come closer!"

E. "Um, what am I doing in here?"

Where can your cat usually be found?

A. Rubbing up against a visitor's legs.

B. Looking out the window pensively.

C. In your lap, purring.

D. Chasing shadows in the hall.

E. Hanging from a tree branch.

When does your cat get the zoomies?

A. When someone throws a toy.

B. Only at night when you're trying to sleep.

C. Never; snuggling is better.

D. 24/7!

E. When leaping from tree to tree.

What does your cat do when you try to rub their belly?

A. Hesitantly accepts the rubs because any attention is good attention.

B. Runs away, horrified.

C. Begs for more.

D. Bunny-kicks the heck outta your hand.

E. Plays dead.

If you mostly answered your cat is . . . **THE LIFE OF THE PURRTY**

Your cat thinks the whole world revolves around them...and it does! They are vocal, confident, and outgoing. They love everyone they meet, and even though you're their favorite, they'll ditch you in a heartbeat to get chin scratches from a visitor. They thrive on interaction and demand your undivided attention.

Tip: Choose enrichment activities that are interactive, like fetch and ribbon dancing!

If you mostly answered your cat is . . . **A DAYDREAMER**

Your cat isn't shy—they're just misunderstood. They might not be the most boisterous kitty in the room, but that's because they're usually deep in thought...or fast asleep! They like to find a good perch where they can post up, observe the world around them, and admire you from a distance.

Tip: Put a tall cat tree in your living room or bedroom so that your cat can enjoy your company from their own safe space!

If you mostly answered your cat is . . . **A CUDDLEBUG**

Personal space is not a concept your cat understands. They're what we call a "needy sweetie" and are happiest when they're being smothered with hugs and kisses! Whether you're relaxing on the couch, doing work at your desk, or simply trying to catch some Zs, your cat truly thinks they need to be right there with you.

Tip: Get your cat a self-grooming brush for some extra love and comfort when you're not around!

If you mostly answered your cat is . . . **A WILD CHILD**

Master of the Butt Wiggle. King of Catnip. Princess of Pouncing. Watch out, world, this cat is ready to rock! Your cat is a playful panther and is constantly zipping around the house turning anything and everything into a toy. This high-energy kitty needs a lot of stimulation in order to tire out, and after a short catnap, they're back at it again!

Tip: Try some battery-operated cat toys that can hold your cat's attention and get out some of their vibrant energy!

If you mostly answered your cat is . . . **AN AWESOME OPOSSUM**

I hate to break it to you, but your cat might be an opossum. No, really. Have you checked for a prehensile tail? If you're certain that this cat is truly a feline, then chances are they're a feral friend who prefers the outdoor life. Feral cats might not want to be indoor companions, but they're every bit as worthy of compassion.

Tip: Make sure the cat is spayed or neutered, and provide daily feedings. Unless they are, in fact, an opossum. In which case...just leave that little cutie alone!

RED LIGHT

GREEN LIGHT

HISS & PURR

Which petting spots does your cat prefer?

Does your cat lean in every time you scratch under their chin? Do they run away when you pat their bare belly? Every feline likes to be touched in a different way, and it's up to us to learn what our cat likes so we can build a trusting and happy relationship with them.

10

BEWARE THE BELLY TRAP Cats may flop on their backs and expose their tummies as a way to show that they're comfortable enough to be vulnerable around you, but that doesn't mean it's an invitation to pet! Proceed with caution and look out for cues like biting, bunny-kicking, or growling—that's their way of saying, "YOU CAN LOOK, BUT YOU CAN'T TOUCH!"

INSTRUCTIONS: Use the color green to indicate your cat's favorite places to be touched. Use the color yellow to indicate the areas where your cat occasionally likes to be touched. Use the color red to indicate the no-go zones!

FELINE FEELINGS

Do you know how to interpret a cat's body language? A few simple cues can tell you if a cat is excited to see you or if they want you to stay away. Here are some feline feelings to look out for.

When cats are **NERVOUS,** they walk low to the ground and look side to side.

When cats are **SCARED,** they crouch down with their tails wrapped around their bodies.

When cats are **RELAXED,** they blink their eyes very slowly.

When cats are **TRUSTING,** they lie with their bellies exposed.

When cats are **DEFENSIVE,** they lower their ears to the sides and hiss.

When cats are **IRRITATED,** they flick their tails back and forth.

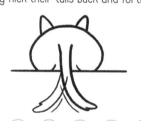

When cats are **HAPPY,** they stick their tails straight up in the air.

When cats are **ATTENTIVE,** they move their ears to listen to the sounds around them.

When cats are **THREATENED,** they arch their backs and puff out their fur.

When cats are **PLAYFUL,** their eyes get wide and they wiggle their butts.

MATCH THE FEELING

Now that you know how to interpret a cat's body language, match the feeling to the cat! WRITE the corresponding number next to each cat to indicate how they are feeling.

1. **RELAXED**
2. **PLAYFUL**
3. **NERVOUS**
4. **DEFENSIVE**
5. **IRRITATED**
6. **SCARED**
7. **HAPPY**
8. **THREATENED**
9. **TRUSTING**
10. **ATTENTIVE**

It's so much fun to think about your cat's persona and what they'd be like as a human. If your cat loves meeting new people and sitting on their laps, then maybe they'd make a purrfect hospitality manager. Or if they love bird-watching from a cozy cat bed in the windowsill, maybe they'd be an excellent wildlife biologist. Maybe it seems silly, but these make-believe activities can be an effective way to describe the personality of your cat or foster animal!

INSTRUCTIONS: Use your imagination to determine the answers to these questions about what your cat would be like as a human.

If your cat had a job, what would it be?

_____

_____

If your cat could talk, what would they say?

_____

_____

_____

_____

What's your cat's dream vacation?

_____

_____

What would be your cat's favorite pizza topping?

_____

What sport would your cat play?

_____

_____

What kind of car would your cat drive?

_____

What kind of animal would your cat have as a pet?

_____

_____

Say your cat was an inventor—
what would they create?

_____

_____

If your cat
wrote a book,
what would the
title be?

_____

_____

_____

If your cat opened a store,
what would they sell?

_____

_____

_____

WRITE AN ODE TO YOUR CAT

LET'S BE HONEST—lots of us sing, cheer, or simply say silly things to our cats. But does your cat have their very own poem or song? Writing in verse is easier than you think! You can even add a simple tune, and then you'll have an adorable jingle you can use to serenade your best feline pal.

First, brainstorm ideas for what you want to write about. You can list your cat's name, nicknames, and 3–5 things that make your cat special, such as physical characteristics, personality traits, and behaviors.

Name:	Ferguson
What makes them special:	Cute, long whiskers, pink nose, acrobatic, loves to jump on me, a little bit of a wild child

Once you have a list, start looking for words with fun rhymes. To make a simple song, you can arrange the rhymes in an **ABCB** format, in which the **B** lines have rhyming words at the end.

EXAMPLE		Now you try. Your ode to your cat doesn't have to be perfect—it can be silly, fun, and ever-changing. The goofier the better!

	EXAMPLE		
A	LITTLE BABY FERGIE-BOY,	A	
B	HOW DID YOU GET SO CUTE?	B	
C	WITH THOSE LONG WHITE WHISKERS	C	
B	AND THAT KISSABLE PINK SNOOT	B	
A	EVEN THOUGH YOU LIKE TO	A	
B	PLAY HOPSCOTCH ON MY HEAD	B	
C	YOU'RE JUST SO DARN PRECIOUS	C	
B	I STILL LET YOU IN MY BED	B	
A	YOU JUMP ON MY SHOULDER	A	
B	LIKE A FLYING ACROBAT	B	
C	AND THAT'S WHY THEY CALL YOU	C	
B	THE AMAZING SUPER-CAT!	B	

CATNAPPIN' DREAMS

The average human sleeps 8 hours each night, but cats have us beat with an amazing average of 12–16 hours of sleep every day. They need to save up all their energy to hunt and play!

Have you ever watched your cat curled up on the couch, deep in slumber? Sometimes cats will wiggle their paws or twitch their ears while they have a catnap, and all we can do is wonder what's happening in their dreams. Are they chasing down a wild buffalo? Climbing to the top of a mountain overlook? Breaking into the treat cabinet?

We may never know, but it sure is fun to imagine what our cats dream about...

INSTRUCTIONS: Draw what you think your cat dreams about in the bubble above.

Learn these different cat colorations by filling in each section with the corresponding color.

White

Colorpoint

Tortie

Black

Dilute Tortie

Some cats carry a recessive allele that makes their fur color appear in its dilute form, making black fur become gray ("blue") and ginger fur become buff. When a tortie appears gray and buff, they're called a *dilute tortie*.

 The allele that produces black fur is dominant, so a cat only needs to get the allele from one parent in order to be a black cat.

1. Green
2. Yellow
3. Blue
4. Pink
5. Black
6. Brown
7. Orange
8. Beige
9. Gray

Tip: If a section doesn't have number, leave it white.

Buff

Bicolor

Tabby

Tuxedo

Calico

Ginger

Only 1 in 3,000 calicos are *male!* A cat must have two X chromosomes in order to be a tricolor cat, which means almost all calicos are female. Most male cats have just one X chromosome, so they can have *either* black fur or orange fur, but almost never both.

LEARN TO DRAW A TERRIFIC TABBY

CONNECT THE DOTS FROM 1 TO 143 TO FILL IN THE CLASSIC PATTERNS OF A TABBY CAT!

DID YOU KNOW EVERY TABBY HAS...

...A TRADITIONAL "M" ON THEIR FOREHEAD,

ISN'T THAT CUTE?

AND A LONG DARK LINE NEXT TO EACH EYE?

A LINE OF LIGHT-COLORED FUR BORDERING THEIR LOWER EYELIDS,

TABBY CAT SCIENCE

Tabby cats have the agouti gene, which causes varying bands of color on each individual strand of fur. Only their distinctive patterns, such as striped legs and an "M" on the forehead, are made up of solid-colored fur. The rest of the fur is multicolored!

Did you know? There are four types of tabbies:

Spotted

Mackerel (Stripes)

Classic (Swirls)

Ticked (No pattern)

FUR REAL

Cats can have lots of different hairstyles—from long, fluffy manes to short and sleek coats.

DRAW YOUR DREAM CAT'S HAIRSTYLE BELOW!

 Cats tend to be meticulous self-groomers, but that doesn't mean they don't benefit from occasional brushing! Brushing your cat helps them have fewer hairballs and less shedding, and it's a great way to provide comfort to your feline friend.

Think you're allergic to cat hair? Think again! People with cats allergies are actually generally allergic to dander (dead skin cells) and a specific protein in cat saliva. Contrary to popular belief, allergies are not better or worse depending on the length of a cat's hair—in fact, even a hairless cat can still produce dander and saliva that can cause allergies. If you think you might be allergic to cats, consider fostering before making the commitment to adopt; adding air filters to your home; and talking to your doctor for advice.

Don't forget to draw their tail!

CAT DETECTIVE

Now that you know all about your cat, it's time to investigate felines outside of your own home. Interview your friends, family members, and other feline-loving people in your life about their cats to see what you can learn.

Person's name: _____

Cat's name: _____

Color pattern: _____

3 words to describe the cat: _____

Favorite place to be pet: _____

Favorite activity: _____

What do you think the cat wants to be when they grow up?

_____

BONUS—Cat's secret name: _____

Person's name: _____

Cat's name: _____

Color pattern: _____

3 words to describe the cat: _____

Favorite place to be pet: _____

Favorite activity: _____

What do you think the cat wants to be when they grow up?

_____

BONUS—Cat's secret name: _____

Person's name: _____

Cat's name: _____

Color pattern: _____

3 words to describe the cat: _____

Favorite place to be pet: _____

Favorite activity: _____

What do you think the cat wants to be when they grow up?

_____

BONUS—Cat's secret name: _____

Person's name: _____

Cat's name: _____

Color pattern: _____

3 words to describe the cat: _____

Favorite place to be pet: _____

Favorite activity: _____

What do you think the cat wants to be when they grow up?

_____

BONUS—Cat's secret name: _____

PLAYTIME & ENRICHMENT FOR CATS

In the wild, cats are surrounded by objects to climb, prey to hunt, endless interesting smells and places to explore...but in our homes, things can be a little ho-hum, because they only have the experiences and environment that we give to them. When caring for a companion cat, it's essential that we provide them with fun toys and items that allow them to live life to the fullest! Playtime enables cats to express their natural hunting instincts, and environmental enrichment can help create a feline wonderland in your home.

In this section, you'll do fun activities that can help cats unleash their inner panther!

Enrichment is any stimulating activity that challenges and satisfies an animal's natural instincts, contributing to their overall physical and psychological wellness.

I SPY CAT TOYS

Cat toys can be lots of fun, but don't just leave them lying on the ground. Where's here's the challenge in that? Playing with a toy that doesn't move is like hunting a mouse that is already dead—it's boring and unlikely to excite your feline friend. Cats love to hunt prey-like items, so they are happiest when you actively play with them and make those toys move!

INSTRUCTIONS: Count all of the cat toys pictured in the image below.

KEY

KICK 'N' GNAW T-SHIRT SPIRALS

The golden rule of playing with your cat is to switch up your routine with new, novel toys and activities. Cats don't want to play with the same crinkle ball every day for the rest of their lives! The good news is you don't have to break the bank to give your cat something new to play with. Many common items in your house can be upcycled into a toy that your cat will adore.

SUPPLIES NEEDED:

Old T-shirt

Toilet paper tube

Scissors

Step 1: Create a long ribbon of fabric by cutting a ½-inch strand off an old T-shirt.

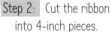

Step 2: Cut the ribbon into 4-inch pieces.

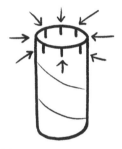

Step 3: Cut 1-inch slits at the top of the toilet paper tube, about 6-10 times each side.

Step 4: Push the frayed ends out.

Step 5: Tightly tie a piece of your T-shirt ribbon around the center and double-knot.

Step 6: Toss and watch your cat enjoy!

BONUS IDEA: FLYING T-SHIRT RIBBON!

Tie a long strand of T-shirt ribbon to a stick and use it as a DIY wand toy. Alternate between waving it in the air and slithering it on the ground to bring out your cat's wild instincts!

TREAT-DISPENSING SQUIGGLY SPIDERS

Cats are natural predators and have a strong urge to act on their hunting instincts. When making a cat toy, try to mimic the things a cat loves about prey. Items that wriggle on the ground or make unpredictable movements will be of top interest. These squiggly spiders offer creepy bug-like legs, an enticing scent, and, best of all, a food reward at the end of the hunt!

SUPPLIES NEEDED:

Toilet paper tube   Pipe cleaners    Your cat's favorite treats    Scissors

Step 1: Pierce 4 tiny holes along one side of the toilet paper tube. Repeat on the opposite side.

Step 2: Cut 2–3 more randomly placed holes, which should be about the size of your cat's favorite treat.

Step 3: Thread a pipe cleaner through each of the 4 sets of holes.

Step 4: Fold one side of the roll inward, sealing off the end.

Step 5: Insert treats and fold the other side inward.

Step 6: Bend the legs to complete your squiggly spider!

BONUS IDEA: SPRINGY SPIRALS!

To make a fun, bug-like spiral, wrap a pipe cleaner around a tubular object like a marker or flashlight and then slide it off. Experiment with a variety of objects for different-sized spirals!

PUZZLE FEEDERS

FOR CATS IN THE WILD, mealtime involves a lot of mental and physical activity—they have to search, hunt, pounce, and attack before they can eat. But for the cats in our house who eat from a dish, dinner can be pretty humdrum and boring. One way to make meals more stimulating for cats is to introduce puzzle feeders into their feeding routine.

Puzzle feeders are objects that turn food time into fun time by encouraging a cat to forage or hunt for their meals. When a cat has to work for their food, it's even more rewarding to chow down!

Some puzzle feeders are stationary, with paw-sized holes that invite the cat to reach in and forage for treats. Other puzzle feeders are movable, with small holes for treats to spill from as the cat bats it around.

You can buy a puzzle feeder from the store...

... or you can make one at home by cutting holes into just about anything that can hold a treat!

 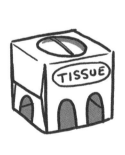 

When you're ready to introduce the puzzle feeder, start by filling it with a handful of enticing treats. Place 1–2 treats on the floor next to the puzzle feeder to get your cat started, then let them "hunt" for the rest!

DIY PUZZLE FEEDER

SUPPLIES NEEDED:

A small cardboard box   2 toilet paper tubes   Hot glue gun and glue   Craft knife

Step 1: Start with a box that is sealed on all four sides.

Step 2: Cut the top ¹/₃ off one of the toilet paper tubes. Now you have small, medium, and large rolls.

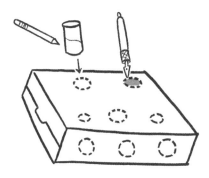

Step 3: Glue each roll to the back of the box.

Step 4: Cut multiple paw-sized holes on each side of the box, making some larger and others smaller.

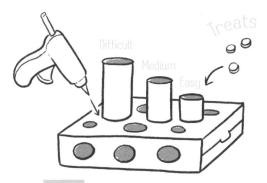

Step 5: Put preferred treats or kibble inside the the box and also inside the treat towers!

 To increase the difficulty of this puzzle feeder, add some loose, crumpled packing paper to the inside of the box to create another obstacle for the cat to overcome!

QUICK TIP!

A muffin tin is a perfect introductory puzzle feeder!
Just add treats and encourage your cat to fish them out.

CARDBOARD CATSLE

We all know that our cats are like royalty, so why not make them a hideaway that's fit for a king or queen? Making a cardboard castle is a fun activity you can do at home, and you can make it as simple or as complex as you'd like.

2 large, sturdy cardboard boxes
Base box minimum size: 15"x15"x15";
Battlement box minimum size: 15"x15"x4"

Scissors

Marker

Hot glue
gun and glue

Tape

Ruler

Step 1: Tape the box flaps shut on both sides of one box. This will be the main level of your castle.

Step 2: Draw your door at the center of the box, ensuring that it's big enough for a cat to enter (Minimum height: 9 inches. Minimum width: 7 inches.) You can choose a rectangular door, a rounded door, or something fun like a cat head shape. Get creative!

Step 3: To make a standard door, cut out the entire shape. Or, to make it a drawbridge, cut everywhere except the bottom and attach a piece of twine to connect the top edges of the cutout and the sides of the box.

Next, cut out a few windows! Choose between round or square—or even some arched windows for a medieval look.

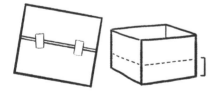

Step 4: Tape the flaps shut on one side of your second box and place the taped end on the floor. Cut the top off the box so that it is 4-6 inches in height. This box will be used for making your battlements!

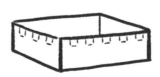

Step 5: Create your battlements by measuring evenly across the top, making a 1.5-inch-long line every 1.5 inches. Cut each line and remove every other flap.

Step 6: Using a hot glue gun and plenty of glue, attach your battlement box to the top of your base box. Now your cat can choose between a cozy hideaway and a scenic lookout!

GREAT JOB!

Now you've got your castle base. From here, there's so much more that you can do to design and decorate your castle. You could...

Create some fun flags using popsicle sticks, colorful construction paper, and a hot glue gun!

Add a blanket inside the battlement box to make a cozy napping spot.

Paint your castle to look like it's made from stone.

Increase the square footage of your castle by adding more boxes to the sides! Cut doorways between the boxes and attach using a hot glue gun.

HAPPY CAMPURR DIY TENT

One thing just about every cat loves is to have a cozy hideaway where they can curl up and get away from it all. You can make a special tent for your cat using simple materials, and pretty soon it'll be your cat's favorite secret napping spot!

SUPPLIES NEEDED:

Old T-shirt

2 wire hangers

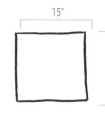

A 15x15" piece of cardboard

Wire cutters

Safety pins

Tape

Step 1: Cut the hooks off the hangers and straighten out the wires.

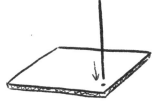

Step 2: Pierce 1 inch of the wire through the cardboard about 1 inch from the edge.

Step 3: Fold the underside of the wire and secure it with tape.

Step 4: With the other end of the wire, pierce the diagonal corner of the cardboard, folding the underside of the wire and securing with tape.

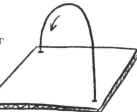

Step 5: Repeat with the other wire.

Step 6: Secure the spot where the 2 wires intersect with tape.

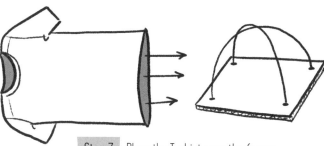

Step 7: Place the T-shirt over the frame, with the neck opening to one side as a door.

UNDERSIDE OF TENT

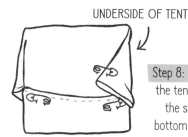

Step 8: Underneath the tent, safety-pin the sleeves and bottom of the shirt.

TA-DA!

Now you have a DIY cat tent! Don't forget to fill it with a soft blanket, toys, or even some treats or catnip.

CAT ADVENTURE

By using a special harness designed for felines, cats can learn to enjoy the great outdoors. Here are some tips for harness-training your cat:

Step 1: Show your cat the harness without putting it on them. Let them sniff it, touch it, and hear what it sounds like. Make it a happy experience with encouraging words and treats.

Step 2: As you slip the harness onto your cat, distract them with treats or a meal to create a positive association. Leave it on for just a minute or two. It's normal if your cat walks funny or tries to escape! Just keep it short and sweet, and make it a positive experience that you repeat several days in a row.

Step 3: Once the cat is comfortable enough to walk in the harness, attach the leash and let them wander around indoors as you follow behind. Keep it quick and repeat for several days.

Step 4: With the harness and leash secure, carry the cat outside and place them into a safe place like a backyard with no other animals around. It's normal for them to feel very overwhelmed and to crouch low at first. If they're uncomfortable, try short spurts of 1-2 minutes for a few days until they become comfortable enough to explore.

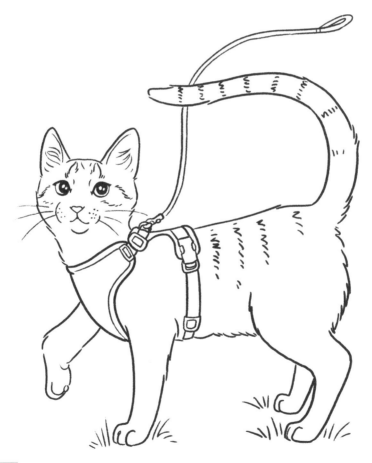

INSTRUCTIONS: Draw some of the things a cat might like to see and explore while on a walk.

Cats don't usually like to walk a straight path or visit public areas with a lot of people and other animals. But they do love to explore quiet areas, watch the birds and butterflies, breathe the fresh air, and soak up the sunshine. Follow your cat's lead, and they'll show you where they'd like to go.

35

COMPLETE THE CATIO

Catios are feline-friendly, screened enclosures that allow a cat to safely experience the outdoors.

These cats can't wait for their catio to be complete! Help them move around the space by adding various components like ramps, steps, perches, bridges, beds, hideaways, and even scratching posts.

BRINGING THE OUTDOORS IN

If you're unable to provide safe outdoor enrichment for your cat, you can always give them a taste of the great outdoors by providing them with elements they might encounter in the wild.

Bring them sticks and leaves (just make sure they're from a nontoxic plant).

Place a pillow in a spot that gets lots of sunlight.

Grow some feline-friendly herbs like catnip, valerian, cat thyme, lemongrass, and chamomile.

Open a window so they can feel the breeze (make sure your window has a secure screen).

Let your cat drink from a faucet or fountain,

Or even put a bird feeder outside a window perch!

GROW YOUR OWN
CAT GRASS

Cats are obligate carnivores who thrive on a diet of meat, so it might surprise you to hear that many cats love to nibble on grass! Wheatgrass, oat grass, barley grass, and ryegrass can be grown individually or together and can be provided as a digestive aid and an enriching snack. Growing cat grass is fun, easy, and quick, so once you follow these simple instructions, your cat will have their very own garden in about one week!

SUPPLIES NEEDED:

Wheat, barley, oat, and/or rye seeds (these grasses can be grown individually or together)

Organic potting soil

A planter with good drainage

Plastic wrap

1. **PREP** Fill your planter with soil. The soil line should be at least an inch below the top of the pot.

2. **SOW** Scatter seeds on top of the soil in a thin layer, then cover them with another ¼ inch of soil.

3. **GERMINATE** Water the soil until moist, then loosely cover the planter in plastic wrap (leave room for air flow) and keep in a warm, dark place for 2-3 days.

4. **GROW** Once the seedlings start to sprout, place the planter in an area with direct sunlight.

5. **WAIT** Allow the grass to grow at least 4-5 inches long before offering it to your cat.

6. **ENJOY!** Once your cat grass is growing, keep it in a sunny spot and water it sparingly—about twice a week. Be sure to sow more seeds regularly so you always have new, fresh cat grass!

BEWARE: Lots of common flowers are toxic to cats! Circle the plants below that are cat safe, and draw an **X** over the plants that are toxic:

See answers on page 117.

ROSE

LILY

GERBERA DAISY

AZALEA

SUNFLOWER

ORCHID

CAT-FRIENDLY
CUPCAKES

Whether you're celebrating a birthday, an adoption anniversary, or any other special occasion, your feline friends will love these healthy, tasty cupcakes for cats! Be sure to choose either a smelly, enticing wet food your cat loves or canned tuna with no spices or flavors added.

CAKE RECIPE

Makes 6 cupcakes

5-oz can of wet cat food or tuna   1 cup oats   ¼ cup hot water   1 egg

1. Combine the canned food, oats, water, and egg in a large bowl and mix well to make a thick batter.

2. Spoon the batter into a cupcake sheet lined with paper baking cups.

3. Bake at 350 degrees F for 15 minutes. Remove from oven and allow to cool before frosting.

ICING RECIPE

1 cup mashed sweet potato
(If using canned sweet potato, be sure that there are no added sugars, spices, or additional ingredients)   2½ oz chicken baby food

1. Line a baking sheet with aluminum foil. Use a fork to poke holes into the sweet potato, then roast at 425 degrees F for 45 minutes. For a faster bake, simply cook the sweet potato in the microwave for 5 minutes.

2. Scoop sweet potato into a bowl with baby food and mash until soft.

TO MAKE FUN DIFFERENT CUPCAKE FLAVORS, TRY ADDING YOUR CAT'S FAVORITE TOPPINGS:

COOKIE CRUMBLE	CATCH OF THE DAY	CAT MINT MADNESS	FISHY DELIGHT	CHEEZYCAKE
(Crushed cat treats)	(Shrimp)	(Catnip)	(Bonito flakes)	(Nutritional yeast)

Always feed your cats treats in moderation, so save these cupcakes for special occasions only! Remember, cats are obligate carnivores who have specific dietary needs that are met by meat-based cat food.

SCRATCHAND

Scratching is an important form of enrichment, comfort, and communication for cats. When a cat scratches an item, the scent glands in their paw pads leave behind a special signal that only cats can smell. It's a special way for them to mark their territory and say, "Ahh, this smells just like home." If your cat is scratching your couch, it's actually a compliment—they're trying to create a happy family scent. Aww! Of course, most of us prefer not to have our couches shredded, so that's why it's always good to offer a post or cat tree that your cat can scratch instead.

DRAW WHAT YOU THINK YOUR CAT WOULD LIKE TO SCRATCH!

DON'T DECLAW

Cats use their claws to climb, stretch, hunt, and defend themselves. Claws are an essential part of their bodies—it's cruel and painful to declaw! Instead, simply trim the tip of your cat's claws with a claw trimmer as needed, and be sure to provide scratching posts.

SNIFF

Cats have 40 times more odor sensors than humans do, making their nose one of their most sensitive and powerful tools for navigating the world around them. When a new smell is present, they may feel curious or excited, sniffing deeply and thinking, *"Whoa—what does this mean?"* One way to give your cat an enriching experience is to expose them to unfamiliar scents. You can spray perfume on a stick, spritz cologne on some packing paper, or even take them on a "scent tour" with household items like (unlit!) candles and condiments.

DRAW SOME THINGS THAT YOUR CAT
MIGHT BE INTERESTED IN SMELLING!

GET A WHIFF OF THIS

Have you ever seen a cat sneer at a strange smell? That's called the flehmen response, and it's a way they investigate a scent through a combination of smelling and tasting. Cats will pause with their mouth agape, allowing the scent to travel to a special organ in the roof of their mouth called the vomeronasal gland, where it can be deeply analyzed.

🐾 HIGH FOUR!

Think tricks are only for dogs? Think again! Cats can learn how to do a variety of tricks on command, and trick training is both an enriching activity for the cat and a wonderful bonding experience for you. A great trick to start with is the high five (or, in the case of cats' paws—'high four!).

STEP 1

Place a treat in your open palm and offer it to your cat. Let your cat eat the treat to spark interest.

STEP 2

Place another treat in your hand, lightly closing your palm. Wait until your cat reaches out to touch your hand with their paw. When they do, say "Good job!" and give them the treat. Repeat.

STEP 3

Gradually begin to lift your hand higher so the cat has to raise their paw to touch your hand. Repeat several times, saying "Good job!" and giving a treat after each touch.

STEP 4

With a treat in your hand at the cat's eye level, say "High five." When your cat reaches out, tell them "Good job!" and give them the treat.

You don't need a clicker for this activity, but if you're interested in teaching your cat more complex tricks, you might want to learn about clicker training. Clicker training is a kind of operant conditioning where the trainer uses a small clicking device to clearly communicate the exact moment that a target behavior is exhibited. Having learned that the click is always followed by a treat, the cat learns to perform different tricks through positive reinforcement. If you don't have a clicker, you can snap, whistle, or even use a phrase like "good job!" Just keep it consistent, and always follow up with a yummy treat.

STEP 5

Lift an empty hand and say "High five!" When they reach out, say "Good job!" and give them a treat. Congratulations—now your cat knows how to give a high five! Be sure to give your cat a treat every time they do a high five to keep them motivated and enriched.

GOOD JOB!

CAT ENRICHMENT BINGO

Every single day, you should try at least one new thing to bring variety into your cat's life. Enrichment doesn't have to be difficult or expensive—many fun activities can be done using items you already have at home. Using the BINGO sheet below, challenge yourself to get five in a row within one week.

BINGO

Move your furniture so that your cat can access a new window view	Play *treat toss* by throwing your cat's favorite treats so they can hunt them	Give your cat crumpled-up packing paper or gift wrap	Create a blanket fort for your cat	Play a special online video made just for cats
Offer your cat a new treat	Make your cat a cardboard castle	Go on a *scent tour* by letting your cat explore different smells around the house	Show your cat what they look like in a mirror	Play the sounds of different wild animals for your cat
Give your cat an empty box	Let your cat drink water slowly dripping from a faucet		Put small toys into a muffin tin for your cat to fish out	Hide cat treats inside an empty tissue box
Teach your cat to give a high five	Wiggle an enticing toy underneath a blanket or sheet	Crinkle up an old receipt or paper note and toss it for your cat	Shine a flashlight on the wall and move it to and fro	Place a bird feeder near a window or play a video of birds
Create an obstacle course with furniture	Freeze an enticing treat, like tuna juice, into fun, lickable ice cubes	Offer your cat catnip or cat grass	Actively play with a wand toy, both in the air and on the ground	Make a treat-dispensing toy out of a toilet paper tube

WHAT WERE YOUR CAT'S FAVORITE ACTIVITIES?

Use this space to create an enrichment journal. Color in the paws from one to five, one meaning they didn't react, and five meaning they had a huge reaction. Make notes on what the reaction was.

ACTIVITY:

_____

_____

_____

_____

_____

_____

_____

ACTIVITY:

_____

_____

_____

_____

_____

_____

_____

ACTIVITY:

_____

_____

_____

_____

_____

_____

_____

RESPONSIBLE FELINE GUARDIANSHIP

There's nothing better than being best friends with a cat! But it's important to know that when you adopt a cat you become not only their pal, but their guardian—and you take on many responsibilities beyond cuddling and playing. Cats depend on us to keep them safe from becoming lost or injured, to keep them healthy through routine veterinary care, and to stay on top of all their needs in the home.

In this section, you'll learn about some of the important duties involved in being a responsible cat caregiver and discover how you can help your best feline friend enjoy a long and healthy life.

Need a hint? See word bank on page 117.

A TRIP TO THE VET
CROSSWORD

When you take your cat to the vet, you're doing your part to ensure that they stay in good health! Veterinarians can help to prevent, diagnose, and treat disease so that your cat can live life to the fullest. Complete the crossword to uncover some of the things you might expect from a trip to the vet!

When should you go to the vet?

- When you adopt a new cat
- When you notice physical symptoms
- When you observe behavioral changes
- Once a year for a checkup and vaccine boosters as needed

1. V E T E R I N A R I A N
10. C

ACROSS

3. activity and movement that keeps your cat healthy
7. documentation of medical care your cat has received
8. every newly rescued kitten should receive ____ to treat for common parasites
10. this important vaccine is required by law in many states
11. if your cat has a respiratory infection, you might be prescribed an ____
12. when your cat is suddenly peeing outside of the box, have him checked for a ____
14. a ____ diet might be recommended for a cat with a medical condition
17. a surgical procedure to sterilize a male cat
18. if a cat has a temperature above 102.5°F, they have a ____
19. a 100% treatable fungal condition affecting the skin, fur, and claws
20. it's recommended to get a ____ cleaning to promote good oral hygiene
22. a veterinarian can give this to your cat to help you find them if they ever get lost
23. every cat should receive an ____ checkup from a vet

DOWN

1. an animal doctor
2. a standard vaccine that protects cats from common viruses
4. an instrument used to listen to a cat's heart
5. if your cat needs a same-day appointment, try to find a walk-in ____
6. a veterinary nurse
9. if your cat has an eye infection, the vet may prescribe a medicated eye drop or ____
13. black specks of dirt in a cat's fur might be a sign of this pest
15. if you see black gunk in your cat's ears, ask your vet to check for these
16. a monthly plan to help cover the cost of your cat's medical care
21. a surgical procedure to sterilize a female cat

49

COLOR THE **COLLAR**

It's important for cats to have a form of identification. One way to do this is to give your cat a collar with a customized tag. On the tag, put your cat's name and contact information. If the cat ever gets lost, a neighbor can look at the tag and know how to help the cat get home.

INSTRUCTIONS: Add fun cat names to the tags, then fill in the collars with your favorite patterns and colors!

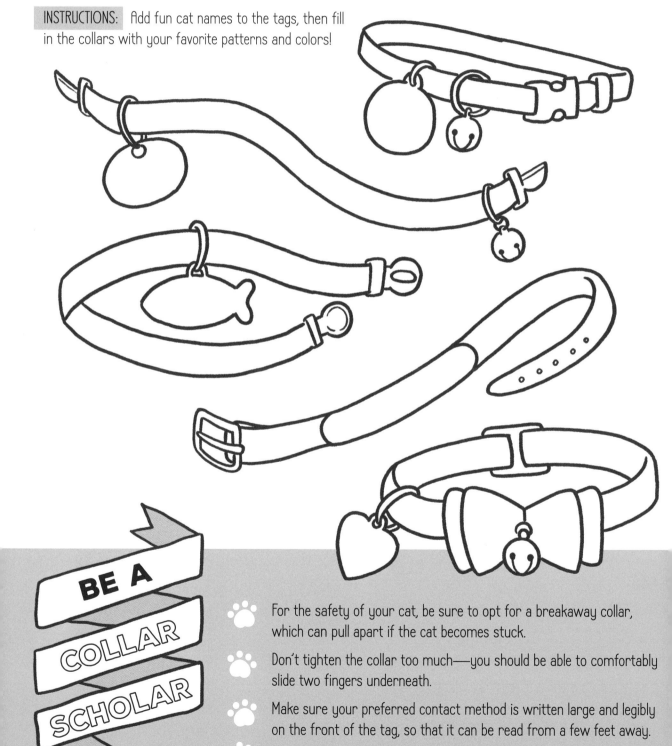

BE A COLLAR SCHOLAR

- For the safety of your cat, be sure to opt for a breakaway collar, which can pull apart if the cat becomes stuck.

- Don't tighten the collar too much—you should be able to comfortably slide two fingers underneath.

- Make sure your preferred contact method is written large and legibly on the front of the tag, so that it can be read from a few feet away.

- If your contact information changes, be sure to get an updated tag!

50

DECODE THE MICROCHIP

Another way to help a cat find their way home is to get them microchipped! A microchip is a small identifying device that is implanted under a cat's skin. These tiny chips are only the size of a grain of rice, but they can make a *big* difference if a cat gets lost.

When a cat is found, a veterinarian or animal shelter employee can wave a scanner over their back to see if they have a microchip. If they do, a long string of numbers will appear on the wand, which is a special code unique to the cat. Using this code, the finder can access contact information for the cat's family—and bring the cat home.

These six lost cats have been found and scanned for a microchip. Decode each microchip number to discover the name of the cat. For each number, write the corresponding letter as it falls alphabetically— 1 = A, 2 = B, 3 = C, and so on.

6 12 21 6 6 25

13 9 19 19   2 9 19 3 21 9 20 19

6 5 18 4 9 14 1 14 4

13 1 18 26 9 16 1 14

18 21 4 15 12 16 8

16 5 15 14 25

DON'T FORGET: A microchip only works if you register it with your contact information. Be sure to keep the microchip up to date any time you move or change your phone number.

CAT CARE CHORE WHEEL

When you adopt a cat, you make a commitment to do a number of routine tasks—from litter scooping to claw trimming. Making a cat care chore wheel is a great way to make sure you're dividing tasks among everyone in the household. With a simple spin of the wheel, you can reassign chores every week, which is sure to keep things fresh for your family (and for your litter box!).

Who is responsible for caring for the cats in your home?

_____

_____

Make a list of cat care responsibilities and their frequency.

TASK	FREQUENCY
Scoop the litter box	Daily
Sanitize the litter box	Weekly
Give medications	As prescribed
Feed	Twice daily
Brush	Weekly
Enrichment and playtime	Twice daily
Trim claws	Every other week
Change the water	Daily

Now choose the responsibilities you want to include in your chore wheel. To ensure the chart works smoothly, make sure there is an equal number of tasks for every person. For instance, if 3 people are sharing responsibilities, you could have 3 tasks, 6 tasks, or 9 tasks.

Colorful construction paper

Metal brad

Marker

Scissors

Step 1: Cut a large circle from a piece of colorful construction paper to create the outer wheel. Using a marker, divide the wheel into the same number of sections as there are people responsible for animal care. Write a name around the edge of each section.

Step 2: Cut a smaller circle from a different color of construction paper to create the inner wheel. Using a marker, divide the wheel into as many sections as there are tasks. Write a task inside each section.

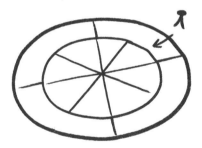

Step 3: Punch a hole into the center of each circle. Attach the small circle to the large circle using the metal brad. Hang the chore wheel somewhere visible, like the refrigerator, and rotate weekly to assign cat care tasks!

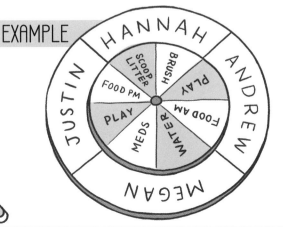

EXAMPLE

JUSTIN HANNAH ANDREW MEGAN

SCOOP LITTER · BRUSH · PLAY · FOOD AM · WATER · MEDS · PLAY · FOOD PM

WHAT'S THE SCOOP ON PEE AND POOP?

LITTER BOX TRIVIA

1. Experts recommend that you have...

A. One litter box for all your cats to share

B. One litter box per cat

C. One litter box per cat, plus one extra

D. Two litter boxes per cat

2. Cats tend to prefer a litter box that is...

A. Hidden in a closet

B. Covered

C. Small

D. Large and uncovered

3. You should scoop the litter box...

A. At least once per day

B. Every other day

C. Once a week

D. Every two weeks

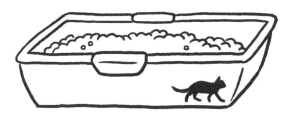

4. When a cat pees outside the box, it's often because...

A. They're being sassy

B. They don't like the color of the litter box

C. They need to see a veterinarian for a urinary issue

D. They just don't like you

5. When a cat gets the "poop zoomies," it's because...

A. They want to run away from the scent as quickly as possible

B. The vagus nerve is stimulated, causing a euphoric feeling

C. They're happy and relieved to be done pooping

D. No one really knows for sure; maybe all of the above!

6. To avoid tummy troubles and problem poop, you should change your cat to a different diet...

    A. Every other week

    B. Every year

    C. By gradually mixing the new food into the old

    D. By offering many options at each meal

7. Kittens start to use the litter box around...

    A. 2 weeks

    B. 4 weeks

    C. 6 weeks

    D. 8 weeks

8. Poop issues can be caused by...

    A. Viruses

    B. Bacteria

    C. Parasites

    D. All of the above

9. The best place to put a litter box is...

    A. In the middle of a room

    B. In the corner of a room

    C. On a table

    D. Under a table

See answers on page 117.

10. The best cat litter for an adult cat is...

    A. Clumping and scented

    B. Non-clumping and unscented

    C. Clumping and unscented

    D. Whatever your cat prefers

SAVE THE DAY
NEUTER AND SPAY

↖ Sassy and Sparky ↗
McDoodle

See answers on page 117.

One of the most important things cat advocates can do is get their feline friends spayed and neutered. Without our help, the cat population grows exponentially so that the number of cats in need outweighs the number of adopters available. By putting an end to the cycle of reproduction, we can decrease the number of cats entering animal shelters and ensure that there are enough loving homes for every cat!

INSTRUCTIONS: Complete the word problems below to learn how quickly a feline family can grow. Tip: Use the blank space under each question to try drawing out every scenario—kitten math can be tricky!

1. Sassy McDoodle and Sparky McDoodle welcome 6 kittens into the world on New Year's Day. How many cats are in their family?

2. At the end of June, 4 of their offspring give birth to 6 more kittens each. How many cats are in the McDoodle family at the end of June?

3. Even though Sassy and Sparky are already grandparents, cats can have multiple litters of kittens in a year...so they welcome another litter of 8 in August! How many cats are in the McDoodle family in August?

4. Whoa! This family is getting big. Of the kittens born in June, 12 give birth to 5 kittens each in early December. How many cats are in the McDoodle family at the end of the year?

5. The local spay/neuter clinic charges $80 per cat for their services. How much will it cost to spay/neuter the McDoodle family in December?

6. How much would it have cost to spay/neuter the McDoodle family in March?

7. How much would it have cost to spay/neuter Sassy and Sparky before they had babies?

8. In mid-December, the McDoodles go to the animal shelter hoping for loving homes. By Christmas, 42 of them are adopted into happy families! How many of them don't find a home by Christmas?

9. If the McDoodles had been spayed/neutered in August, how many of them would still be looking for a home by Christmas?

DON'T DELAY—SCHEDULE THAT SPAY!
SPAYING AND NEUTERING SAVES LIVES!

SPAY & NEUTER
TRUE OR FALSE?

TRUE OR FALSE:

The only way to experience caring for kittens is to let your cat have babies.

FALSE! Animal shelters are filled with kittens who need a safe place to go. Rather than contribute to overpopulation, try signing up as a foster parent so you can care for kittens whenever you want—and save their lives, too.

TRUE OR FALSE:

Neutering a cat will change his personality.

This is TRUE, but only insofar as he won't have an urge to fight, mate, or spray all the items in your house. Neutering doesn't have any negative impact on your cat's playfulness or cuddliness—it simply makes him less stinky and territorial. Yay!

TRUE OR FALSE:

Kittens can't be spayed or neutered until they are at least 6 months old.

Oh boy, this is definitely FALSE! Kittens can be safely spayed or neutered once they reach 2 pounds and 2 months of age. Remember, kittens can get pregnant as early as 4 months of age, so don't delay; schedule a spay.

TRUE OR FALSE:

Spayed and neutered cats live healthier, longer lives.

TRUE! Spaying and neutering reduces or eliminates the risk of certain cancers and life-threatening infections. Spayed female cats live an average of 39% longer, and neutered males live an average of 62% longer.

CHOMP CHOMP

Learn about feline dental health with these cat tooth facts!

- Kittens have 26 baby teeth, and adult cats have 30 permanent teeth.

- Studies show that more than 50% of cats over the age of 4 suffer from some form of dental disease. Dental disease can cause pain, inflammation, drooling, and discomfort while eating.

- Pee-yew! Bad breath can be a sign of dental disease. If your cat's breath has a funky smell, head to the vet for a dental exam. Your veterinarian can do a sedated dental cleaning to keep your cat's teeth in good health.

- Yes! You can brush a cat's teeth. Choose a special cat-safe toothpaste and toothbrush, and start by letting them lick some of the paste from your finger, then from the brush. It may take several sessions over several weeks, but gradually you can teach your cat to accept toothbrushing! Never use human toothpaste, as it can contain ingredients that are toxic to cats.

INSTRUCTIONS: Complete the drawing of the open-mouthed cat by mirroring the lines.

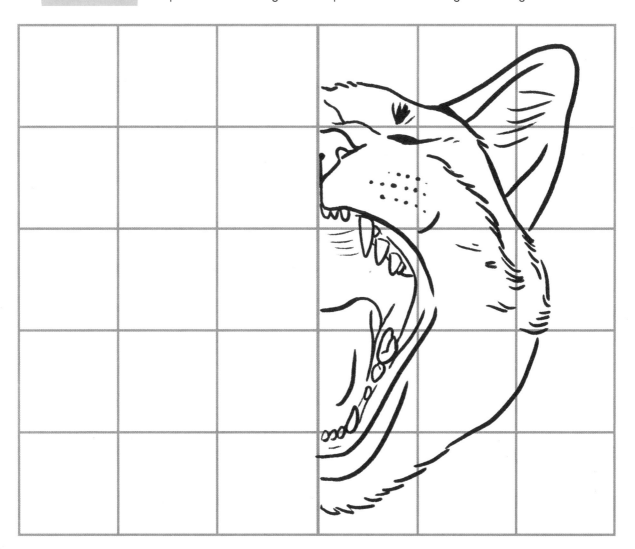

HELPING COMMUNITY CATS

Have you ever spotted a crew of cats living outside in your neighborhood? These independent, free-roaming felines are called community cats, and they live outdoors in family groups called colonies. While these cats can have a range of personalities and experiences, it's common for them to be feral or under-socialized due to their lack of experience interacting with humans. They may not prefer to live indoors, but we can still show them we care by providing them with food, outdoor shelter, and vaccination—and, most importantly, by getting them spayed and neutered in order to stop the cycle of reproduction.

In this section, you'll learn all about the wonderful world of feral felines and community cats and find out how you can make a difference for the cats living beyond your doorstep.

EARTIP ♥ LOVE

When you see cats in your neighborhood, you should always look for an eartip. An eartip is a universal sign that a community cat has been spayed or neutered!

Eartips are a sign of love. They signal that a compassionate person has humanely trapped the cat, had them vaccinated and spayed/neutered, and returned them to their territory.

WHY EARTIP?

Eartipping is done painlessly while under anesthesia for spay/neuter surgery. The cat doesn't lose any function at all, but gains a world of protection. Eartips are the best form of identification for sterilized community cats because:

🐾 They're easy to see in the dark and from a distance.

🐾 They help cat rescuers know who still needs to be trapped and who doesn't.

🐾 They prevent cats from being needlessly brought to the shelter or spay/neuter clinic. Think of it like a hall pass for cats who live outside!

TRAP THE CAT

Spaying and neutering isn't just for companion cats! Community cats also rely on us to help them get vaccinated and spayed or neutered through a process called

TRAP-NEUTER-RETURN (TNR)!

TNR helps save the lives of free-roaming cats, while also reducing the number of kittens entering animal shelters. If you're a cat lover, one of the most meaningful things you can do is help community cats access sterilization. Follow these steps to learn how to trap the cats in your neighborhood for TNR:

🐾 Make an appointment with a spay/neuter clinic that helps community cats.

🐾 Gather supplies like humane traps, large towels, a tarp, and smelly cat food. Ask your local shelter or cat rescue group if they have traps you can borrow.

DRAW SOME FOOD ITEMS YOU THINK WOULD MAKE GOOD BAIT:

🐾 Talk to neighbors in the area. Get permission if you want to trap on their property, and ask them not to feed the cats the day before (you'll want them to be hungry). Ask questions that can help you successfully catch the cats, like:

Do you know where the cats like to hang out?

Who might be feeding the cats?

What time of day do you usually see them?

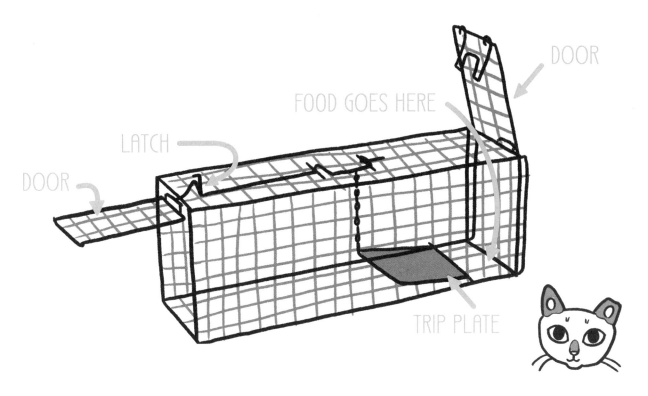

DOOR

LATCH

FOOD GOES HERE

DOOR

TRIP PLATE

Strategically set the traps in the area. When a cat smells the delicious food, they can't resist entering. They step on the trip plate, which closes the door gently behind them and encloses them in the trap.

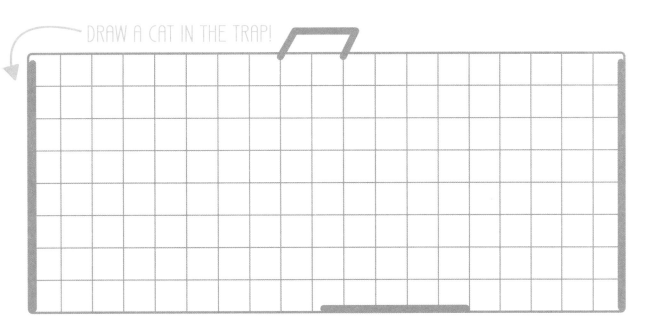

DRAW A CAT IN THE TRAP!

Cover the trap with a large towel and bring them to the spay/neuter appointment. Then, 24 hours after surgery, they can be returned to the exact location where they were found.

After you trap the cats in your neighborhood, they can continue on with their lives without the population growing out of control. Woo-hoo!

COMMUNITY CAT SEEK & FIND

Free-roaming cats are called "community cats" because they are truly a part of the community! They tend to live in densely populated areas, such as neighborhoods and cities, where there are resources like food, water, and shelter. Some may live in managed colonies, while others may be solitary. Some may be quite visible, while others may be more hidden.

TRY TO SPOT ALL THE COMMUNITY CATS IN THIS PICTURE!

See answers on page 117.

Next time you're out and about, see if you can spot any community cats in your neighborhood. Don't forget to check for eartips!

How many community cats can you find?

How many of the cats have eartips?

How many of the cats still need to be spayed or neutered?

NEIGHBORHOOD WATCH

Do you notice cats walking around your neighborhood? Start to keep notes on who you see, and pay attention to whether or not they have an eartip. If a cat doesn't have an eartip, it's a good idea to make a plan for TNR! Keeping track of the cats is a great place to start.

CAT #1

COLOR/DESCRIPTION:————————————————

AGE:	KITTEN	ADULT	SENIOR
COLLAR:	YES	NO	
EARTIP:	YES	NO	

AREA TYPICALLY SEEN: ————————————————

NOTES:————————————————

CAT #2

COLOR/DESCRIPTION: ————————————————

AGE:	KITTEN	ADULT	SENIOR
COLLAR:	YES	NO	
EARTIP:	YES	NO	

AREA TYPICALLY SEEN: ————————————————

NOTES: ————————————————

CAT #3

COLOR/DESCRIPTION: _____

AGE: KITTEN   ADULT   SENIOR

COLLAR: YES   NO

EARTIP: YES   NO

AREA TYPICALLY SEEN: _____

NOTES: _____

_____

_____

CAT #4

COLOR/DESCRIPTION: _____

AGE: KITTEN   ADULT   SENIOR

COLLAR: YES   NO

EARTIP: YES   NO

AREA TYPICALLY SEEN: _____

NOTES: _____

_____

_____

CAT #5

COLOR/DESCRIPTION: _____

AGE: KITTEN   ADULT   SENIOR

COLLAR: YES   NO

EARTIP: YES   NO

AREA TYPICALLY SEEN: _____

NOTES: _____

_____

_____

 Of course, if a cat has a collar, it's likely they are a companion cat! Look at the identifying information on their tag and find out whether they are lost or are just an indoor/outdoor cat.

69

ORIGAMI CAT COLONY

SUPPLIES NEEDED: Origami paper (2 sheets per cat) · Markers

SHEET ONE

Step 1: Start with the paper colored side down and with one point facing you, like a diamond.

Step 2: Fold the top corner down to the bottom corner to make a triangle.

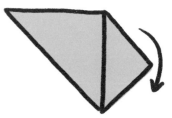

Step 3: Fold the side points down to meet the bottom point, forming a diamond shape with two flaps.

Step 4: Fold the flaps up, slightly over the edge, to form the ears.

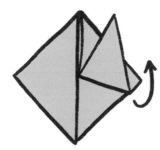

Step 5: Fold the top point down to the center of the two flaps.

Step 6: Flip the entire project to the other side, and you should have a cat head with a pointy chin!

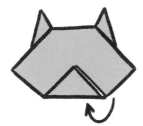

Step 7: Fold both sections at the bottom point up to meet the middle of the head.

Step 8: Lift the top flap and hide the back flap behind it.

Step 9: Fold the tip of the top flap down to form the nose.

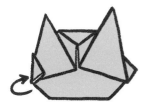

Step 10: Fold the cheeks back slightly to round out the face. Now you have your cat head!

Next, make the body and complete your cat!

Step 11: Start with the paper colored side down and with a flat side facing you, like a square.

Take the upper right point and fold it down to meet the lower left point.

Step 12: Fold the right corner in ¾ of the way to make the tail. Now you have the cat's body!

Step 13: Unfold the top of the cat's head.

Place the pointy top of the cat's body between the two sections at the bottom of the cat head until the body point is inside the head point.

Fold the top point down again to secure the body to the head.

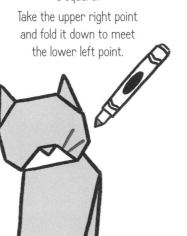

Step 14: Use your markers to add eyes, whiskers, or even fur coloration.

Repeat the steps to make more friends for your cat.

Now that your cat colony is complete, there's just one more thing to do—add eartips by folding one ear back on each cat!

An eartip is a sign that a community cat has been trapped, sterilized, and provided for by a caring person.

EARTIPS = LOVE!

DIY WINTER SHELTERS
FOR COMMUNITY CATS

If you live in an area with chilly weather, one great way to help the cats in your neighborhood is to make some winter shelters. Using simple materials, you can create an insulated hideaway for your backyard, porch, or alley and provide a safe space for the free-roaming felines in your community!

SUPPLIES NEEDED:

Large (30–32 gallon) plastic storage bin

Medium (20–22 gallon) plastic storage bin

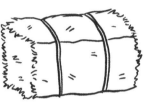

Straw

Craft knife

Marker

4"

Step 1: On the shorter end of the large bin, use the marker to draw a circular doorway with a 6-inch diameter. To prevent flooding, make sure that the bottom of the circle is at least 4 inches from the bottom of the bin. Carefully cut out the circle using a craft knife.

Step 2: Add a layer of straw to the bottom of the bin.

TIP!
Warming the plastic bin with a hair dryer can make it easier to cut.

Step 3: Place the medium bin inside the large bin and trace the circular doorway. Carefully cut out the circle using a craft knife.

Step 4: Insulate the shelter by stuffing straw between the medium and large bins on all sides. Add straw to the inside of the medium bin for cozy bedding.

TIP!

Don't use insulating materials that absorb moisture, like blankets, towels, or newspaper. Even hay is not ideal, because it holds moisture and can become moldy. Straw is a better option, because it stays nice and dry!

Step 5: Place the lid on the medium bin, add more straw on top of it, and place the lid on the large bin.

Step 6: Now that your winter shelter is complete, place it in a discreet, secure, safe area away from predators. Don't place the shelter near where the cats are fed, as this may attract unwanted animal visitors that make the cat less likely to use it. Face the entrance toward a wall to protect from wind, rain, and snow.

IF YOU LIVE IN A VERY COLD AREA, FOLLOW THESE EXTRA STEPS:

🐾 Don't place the shelter directly on the cold ground; placing it on a wood platform is better.

🐾 Consider using Styrofoam insulation in between the bins for extra warmth.

FRIENDLY OR FERAL ?

Feral is a term used to describe a cat who is unsocialized to humans. Feral isn't synonymous with mean or vicious; it simply means these cats have not had much exposure to humans and are therefore uncomfortable around them. Feral cats may exhibit avoidant or defensive behaviors when approached, so it's important to respect them and not force them to interact. Of course, feral cats deserve consideration and protection, just like their more social feline pals—even if they don't want to snuggle us!

Community cats can be friendly, feral, or anywhere in between. Socialization is a spectrum, and friendliness varies from cat to cat based on their early experiences. When you encounter a community cat, it will be helpful to determine whether they're friendly or feral using some of these telltale signs.

INSTRUCTIONS: Complete the cat drawings to show the differences between friendly and feral behaviors.

FRIENDLY	FERAL

MEOWING

HAPPY WHEN APPROACHED

GROWLING

HISS WHEN APPROACHED

TAIL IS UPRIGHT

FUR IS FLAT

TAIL WRAPPED TIGHT
AGAINST BODY

FUR MAY BE
POOFED OUT

EARS UPRIGHT

PUPILS NORMAL

EARS FLATTENED

PUPILS DIALATED

KITTEN LOST AND FOUND

Oh dear, a baby kitten was found outside all alone. But don't panic—their mama is probably right around the corner. Let's leave the kitten right where they are and help the mama find her way back to her baby.

INSTRUCTIONS: Starting at the mama cat, draw a line to follow the path to her kitten. Just be careful and don't let the cat get distracted by any treats along the way...

ARE YOU MY MOM?

When a kitten is found outside, the first thing you should do is try to locate the mother. Which of these cats do you think might be the missing mama? Why? When you find her, draw a line from the mama to the kitten.

Once you've identified a kitten's mama, you can reunite them outdoors or in foster care. Kittens do best when they live with their mother until they are old enough to be weaned. Mama cats provide warmth, nutrition, grooming, protection, and love.

See answer on page 117.

SAVING THE TINIEST FELINES

Baby kittens are born vulnerable and defenseless, relying on their mamas for everything from food to protection to potty assistance. Newborns are unable to do much on their own aside from sleep, nurse, and purr... so when these little ones end up in an animal shelter, they need compassionate people like you and me to step up and lend a hand! Foster parents are everyday superheroes who open their homes to kittens and help with their care, feeding, and socializing until they are old enough to go to their forever homes.

In this section, you'll learn all about the development and care of kittens and how you can make a big difference for the littlest felines.

HOW KITTENS GROW:
FROM BIRTH TO ADOPTION!

They're frail and defenseless
when they're 1 week old.
They cuddle for warmth so
that they don't get cold.

A small newborn kitten
can't see you or hear.
They nurse all day long
and keep the mama cat near.

By 2 weeks of age,
they first open their eyes.
They can't wander far,
being so small in size.

When they reach week 4
they start wanting to play.
They pounce on their toys
like they're hunting for prey.

They get their first baby teeth
in by week 3.
By this age they walk,
they can hear and can see.

They get all their baby teeth in by week 5,
They wean onto meat, which they need to survive.

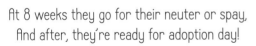

At 8 weeks they go for their neuter or spay,
And after, they're ready for adoption day!

A 7-week-old loves
to climb, jump, and run.
They're packed full of spunk
and they love to have fun.

At 6 weeks their eyes still
have some baby blue,
but their adult eye color
starts coming through.

KITTEN MILESTONE TIMELINE

One of the most rewarding parts of fostering is getting to watch little kittens grow bigger and stronger every day. Each new milestone a kitten reaches brings them closer to the moment when they can find their forever home!

How well do you know your kitten developmental milestones? Write the corresponding letters on the timeline to decode the most important milestone of all!

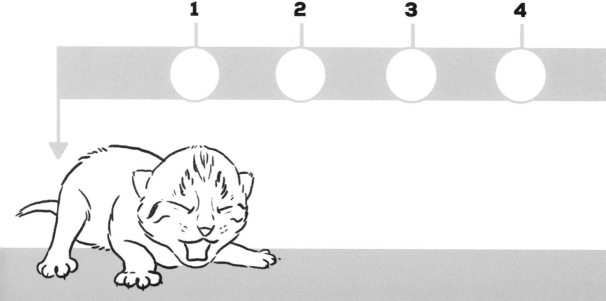

1   2   3   4   5

T WEANING ONTO MEAT

! CAN BE SPAYED OR NEUTERED

P STARTING TO PLAY WITH TOYS

D CAN CLIMB CONFIDENTLY

A UNABLE TO SEE OR HEAR

O FIRST BABY TEETH EMERGE

D OPENS EYES FOR THE FIRST TIME

E ADULT EYE COLOR EMERGES

6   7   8

See answer on page 117.

GOTCHA DAY!

WHAT'S THE WEIGHT?

During the first weeks of life, caregivers weigh kittens every single day to ensure that they are growing and on track. Each day, a healthy kitten will gain 7–14g. By keeping a written log, you can ensure that a kitten is steadily growing without issue. Between birth and adoption age, kittens will grow more than 10 times in size! Kittens can be as small as 75g (or sometimes even less) at birth and will reach 907g (2 pounds) before they are spayed or neutered and placed in a forever home.

Bartholomew: 687g
Intake weight: 325g

Beep: 534g
Intake weight: 82g

Doodle: 454g
Intake weight: 120g

1) Which kitten has gained the most weight since intake?

_____

2) Which kitten has gained the least weight since intake?

_____

3) Which kitten is the closest to reaching 2 pounds?

_____

Note: 453.5 grams = 1 pound.

Meep: 111g
Intake weight: 90g

Ronald: 499g
Intake weight: 290g

Angela: 143g
Intake weight: 88g

4) Which kitten is the furthest from reaching 2 pounds?

_____

5) Which two kittens are the closest to each other in weight?

_____

6) Which kitten recently hit the 1-pound mark?

_____

Need a hint? See answers on page 117.

KITTEN ANATOMY FILL IN THE BLANKS

It's no secret that fostering kittens can make you go absolutely gaga. Before you know it, you're baby-talking, singing lullabies, and making up all sorts of silly words in an attempt to describe their unbelievable cuteness. Instead of calling it a nose, you start calling it their **"snootle-mcdoodle,"** and their paw pads suddenly become their **"jellybean twinkle-toes!"**

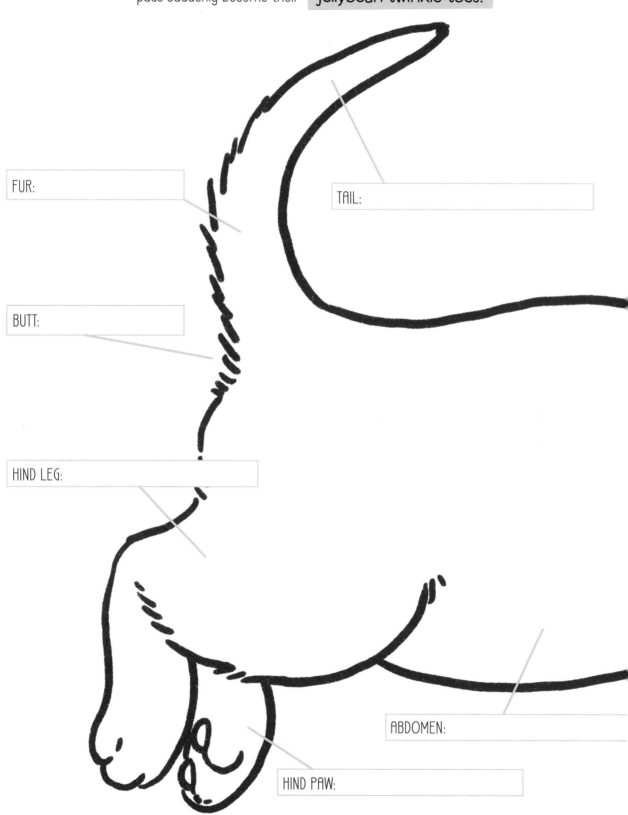

FUR:

TAIL:

BUTT:

HIND LEG:

ABDOMEN:

HIND PAW:

EXAMPLE: MUZZLE: _____cheekypuffs_____

EAR:

NOSE:

PRE-MOLARS:

MUZZLE:

WHISKERS:

CANINE:

TONGUE:

INCISORS:

DIGITAL PADS:

PAW:

CLAWS:

BONUS: **COLOR THE KITTY WITH YOUR FAVORITE CAT FUR COLOR PATTERN**

87

KITTEN NURSERY
SPOT THE DIFFERENCES!

How many differences can you spot between the two nurseries?

Newborn kittens, also called neonatal kittens, need special care and supplies to help them thrive during their first weeks of life. Kitten foster parents make a lifesaving difference by opening their homes to little ones in need of a temporary place to go. A foster home can provide warmth, comfort, cleaning, and around-the-clock feeding to the littlest felines.

While all kittens have similar needs, there are many different setups that can help them! No two foster homes are exactly alike.

89

IT'S TIME TO GO TO THE KITTEN SHOWER!

A kitten shower is a fun party to celebrate the joy of fostering kittens, and each guest chips in and brings a gift the little ones can enjoy! Which gift will you bring?

Find 15 kitten supply ideas in the word search below, then pick which one you'd like to bring as a gift.

```
K W I N D O W P E R C H I
I E N R I C H M E N T G C
B T H L I T T E R F J H A
B F O R M U L A S E B I T
L O C B A H E A T P A D T
E O B A O B D M V T B E R
T D C W T T R I E L Y A E
R M X D L T A S U W W E
E U N P T C O L I H I A C
A E O N O E K Y E R P Y P
T O O T H B R U S H E I C
S C R A T C H E R S S A B
```

WINDOWPERCH	FORMULA	WET FOOD
TREATS	HEATPAD	BOTTLE
SCRATCHER	CAT TOYS	BABYWIPES
KIBBLE	LITTER	HIDEAWAY
ENRICHMENT	TOOTHBRUSH	CAT TREE

MY KITTEN SHOWER GIFT:

The PURRINCE and PURRINCESS of FOSTERLAND

HOW TO MAKE A CROWN OR HENNIN FOR YOUR FOSTER KITTEN

When a kitten is preparing to search for their forever home, one fun way to promote them to prospective adopters is to pop a tiny hat on their head for a photo! A tiny crown or hennin is a great way to show people that your foster kitten deserves—and demands—to be treated like royalty.

SUPPLIES NEEDED:

Construction paper

Scissors

Hot glue gun and glue

OPTIONAL:

Poof balls
Sticky gems
Fabric
Toilet paper

TO MAKE YOUR CROWN

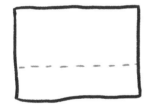

Cut a 1.5" x 4" rectangle out of a piece of construction paper and cut at least 5 pointy triangles into one of the long sides. Glue the ends together to make your crown.

TO MAKE YOUR HENNIN

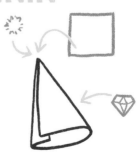

To make your hennin, cut a 3" x 3" rounded arc out of the corner of a piece of construction paper. Glue the long straight ends together to create your cone. Cut a 3" x 3" square of fabric or toilet paper and glue one corner to the top of the cone.

Complete the look with a poof ball and sticky gems around the base!

2 KITTENS ARE BETTER THAN 1

Kittens do best when they have a playmate! When adopting a little one, it's a good idea to consider a pair—especially if you don't already have a cat at home. Adopting a duo helps the kittens stay happy, healthy, and active, and it eases the transition into a new home. It's so rewarding to watch bonded kittens grow up together and stay best friends forever.

INSTRUCTIONS: This litter of 6 has 3 adopters. Which kittens would you pair together, and which adopter would you send them home with? Write their adopter number on the line beside each kitten.

ADOPTER 1
A big family with kids, looking for a playful and friendly duo

ADOPTER 2
A sweet couple with one cat, looking for two cuddly kittens

ADOPTER 3
An active man, looking for a pair of kittens who might like to go on adventures

PANCAKE

Pancake is a laid-back buff baby with stunning green eyes. He keeps his coat impeccably groomed, and he even likes to groom other cats—including his brothers, sisters, and the cats who live in his foster home.

ADOPTER _____

WAFFLE

This outgoing tabby boy is full of energy and needs lots of attention! He just wants someone to play fetch with, or to toss his favorite mouse toy...and he loves having a kitten friend to pounce on and chase.

ADOPTER
_____

BLUEBERRY

Blueberry is a curious blue girl who is fascinated by the outdoors and loves to watch the birds through the window. She loves to roam and explore, and would do great on a harness!

ADOPTER _____

BANANA

When Banana the calico has a sibling by her side, there's no place she won't go! She loves to trot alongside her littermates and investigate new settings.

ADOPTER _____

CHOCOLATE CHIP

Chocolate Chip is a snuggly, silky-smooth black kitten who loves to curl up on the couch for movie time. She loves to be groomed by her siblings, and adores other cats!

ADOPTER _____

MAPLE

Maple is an outgoing orange boy who craves interaction and playtime. He would love to be adopted with an energetic sibling he can tumble around the house with!

ADOPTER _____

MAKING A DIFFERENCE FOR CATS IN NEED

More than 3 million cats enter United States shelters every year—and they are counting on compassionate people like us to do our part to advocate for them! Of course, one of the very best ways to show that you love cats is to adopt one from a nearby animal shelter or rescue group and give them a loving forever home. But even if you can't adopt, there are so many other ways you can chip in by volunteering, donating, or lending your special skills to local organizations that help cats.

In this section, you'll learn about the adoption process and uncover the many ways you can use your passions and talents to help save cats. When we all do a little, together we can do a lot!

COZY CAT BLANKETS

Cat blankets provide warmth and comfort for the felines in our homes, but what about all the cats in animal shelters who don't have a home just yet? One of the ways we can take action for cats is to donate items like blankets and beds, which can help shelter cats feel the comfort of home even while they are waiting to meet their forever families. Making cat blankets for your local shelter is fun and easy, and the cats will be so grateful to have a comfy place to rest!

SUPPLIES NEEDED:

Scissors

Fleece fabric in at least 2 colors

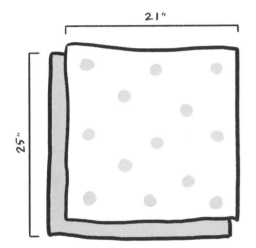

Step 1: Place 2 pieces of fleece back-to-back and cut both to be 25" x 21".

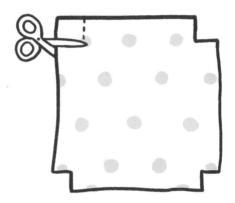

Step 2: Cut a 3" square from each corner.

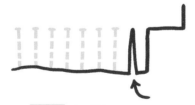

Step 3: Cut 3"-long strips every 1" on each side.

Step 4: Separate the layers of each strip and tie them together in a knot.

TA-DA!

Not sure where to donate? Hop online and look up "animal shelter" or "cat rescue" plus the name of your city. Call them and let them know you'd like to drop off some cozy cat blankets!

THE PURRFECT MATCH

When you go to the animal shelter, you'll meet so many different adoptable kitties looking for homes. An adoption counselor will ask you some questions to get to know you and to help you pick a companion. While it's important to keep an open mind and let the cat choose you, it's also a great idea to think about what kind of cat might be the best fit for your home and lifestyle. Answer these questions to find your purrfect match!

Follow the path to find the right cat for you!

START HERE!

I already have a cat at home

YES — **NO**

A KITTEN

I currently have...

AN ADULT

I'd love to have a high-energy household

YES — **NO**

YES

I'm pretty sure I want to have a one-cat household long term

I'M OPEN TO TWO

I would describe my cat as young and playful

It's okay with me if my toes get munched on occasionally

YES — **NO**

NO

But I really want a kitten

I really want someone to...

PLAY WITH — **CUDDLE**

I spend a lot of time away from home

It's important that I know a lot about what the cats personalities will be long-term

YES — **NO**

NO — **YES**

NO — **YES**

YES — **NO, I'M FLEXIBLE**

Consider adopting...
A KITTEN!

Consider adopting...
AN ADULT CAT!

Consider adopting...
A SENIOR CAT!

Consider adopting...
A BONDED PAIR OF ADULTS OR SENIORS!

Consider adopting...
TWO KITTENS!

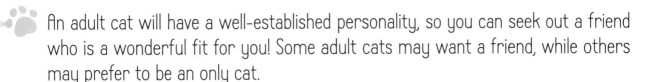 An adult cat will have a well-established personality, so you can seek out a friend who is a wonderful fit for you! Some adult cats may want a friend, while others may prefer to be an only cat.

There's nothing sweeter than giving a precious senior cat a warm lap and a loving home during their golden years. These mellow cats will melt your heart with their grateful purrs.

Bonded pairs can have a difficult time finding homes together—so if you're ever considering two cats, it's a great idea to simply adopt a bonded pair and keep their feline friendship alive!

First-time adopters should know that two kittens are half the work of one (and twice the joy!). A pair of kittens might also be a good fit for a home with an adult cat; the kittens can enjoy each other's company without pestering the original cat.

THE ROAD TO ADOPTION

BORN IN AN ALLEY

TAKEN TO THE VETERINARIAN

BROUGHT TO AN ADOPTION EVENT

FED BY A LOCAL CAREGIVER

SURRENDERED TO AN ANIMAL CONTROL OFFICER

PLACED IN A FOSTER HOME

TAKEN IN TEMPORARILY BY A NEIGHBOR

BROUGHT TO INTAKE AT AN ANIMAL SHELTER

HOUSED IN CAT ROOM AT THE SHELTER

Each shelter cat has their own unique journey to adoption, with lots of different people who may help along the way! It takes a village to help cats, and every small act of kindness and support helps a cat get closer to where they belong.

Follow along the path from birth to adoption, and write the numbers 1–10 next to each step!

See answers on page 117.

ADOPTED INTO A LOVING FOREVER HOME!

ADOPTION SHOPPING LIST

Before you bring home a new feline friend, make sure you've purchased all the supplies you'll need in order to give them a comfortable home.

INSTRUCTIONS: Find 14 items to add to your shopping list!

W	A	T	E	R	F	O	U	N	T	A	I	N	V
S	C	R	A	T	C	H	I	N	G	P	O	S	T
W	A	N	D	T	O	Y	C	C	J	F	C	F	L
W	B	L	U	K	V	P	M	L	A	I	R	V	I
K	P	M	T	D	T	R	E	A	T	S	I	S	T
G	V	W	H	H	J	M	O	W	U	P	N	G	T
T	D	I	S	H	E	S	L	T	D	F	K	U	E
U	I	F	P	J	D	E	T	R	F	A	L	J	R
A	H	A	R	N	E	S	S	I	O	K	E	E	B
C	U	C	A	T	B	E	D	M	O	L	B	H	O
S	C	O	O	P	E	R	Z	M	D	U	A	X	X
G	N	T	C	A	R	R	I	E	R	X	L	R	E
Y	I	S	N	S	Q	M	F	R	N	L	L	F	Y
C	A	T	T	R	E	E	Z	S	H	B	S	J	Y

CLAW TRIMMERS   WAND TOY   SCOOPER

CAT BED   DISHES   CAT TREE

SCRATCHING POST   CARRIER   CRINKLE BALLS

FOOD   LITTER BOX   HARNESS

WATER FOUNTAIN   TREATS

ADOPT ME!

Adoption profiles are an important way for prospective adopters to learn a bit about the different cats who are seeking a forever home. No two cats are alike—so every biography is unique! Help complete the adoption profiles below by filling in the blanks with the designated parts of speech.

A
1. NAME
2. NUMBER BETWEEN 1 AND 10
3. VERB
4. ADJECTIVE
5. COLOR
6. COLOR
7. ADJECTIVE
8. BODY PART
9. VERB ENDING IN -ING
10. ANIMAL
11. VERB ENDING IN -ING
12. PROFESSION
13. ADJECTIVE
14. ADJECTIVE

B
1. SIZE
2. NAME
3. ADJECTIVE
4. VERB ENDING IN -ING
5. ANIMAL
6. COLOR
7. ADJECTIVE
8. COLOR
9. TYPE OF FABRIC
10. ADJECTIVE
11. OBJECT
12. NUMBER BETWEEN 10 AND 20
13. EMOTION

C
1. NAME
2. NAME
3. ADJECTIVE
4. COLOR
5. OBJECT
6. OBJECT
7. DESSERT
8. VERB
9. VERB
10. VERB
11. VERB
12. FURNITURE
13. TYPE OF VEHICLE
14. ADJECTIVE

A Look out, world,—it's ____(1. NAME)____ ! This ____(2. NUMBER BETWEEN 1 AND 10)____ -year-old cat is ready to ____(3. VERB)____ his way into your heart. He has a ____(4. ADJECTIVE)____ ____(5. COLOR)____ coat and ____(6. COLOR)____ eyes, but his most stunning feature is his ____(7. ADJECTIVE)____ ____(8. BODY PART)____ . When he's not catching up on a catnap, he's ____(9. VERB ENDING IN -ING)____ around the house like a ____(10. ANIMAL)____ . He can even do tricks, like ____(11. VERB ENDING IN -ING)____ ! In a past life, he was probably a ____(12. PROFESSION)____ , because he's just so darn ____(13. ADJECTIVE)____ . If you're looking for a ____(14. ADJECTIVE)____ friend to cuddle, he just might be your guy.

B This ____(1. SIZE)____ lady is ____(2. NAME)____ , and she has lots of love to give! She likes long naps on ____(3. ADJECTIVE)____ laps, ____(4. VERB ENDING IN -ING)____ in the sunshine, and playing wth her stuffed ____(5. ANIMAL)____ . You'll be mesmerized by her ____(6. COLOR)____ eyes and her ____(7. ADJECTIVE)____ ____(8. COLOR)____ fur, which feels softer than ____(9. TYPE OF FABRIC)____ . Not only does she keep herself looking ____(10. ADJECTIVE)____ , but she'll also lick your face and groom you until you look prettier than a ____(11. OBJECT)____ . She's ____(12. NUMBER BETWEEN 10 AND 20)____ years young and ready to fill your heart with ____(13. EMOTION)____ , so fill out an adoption application today!

C You won't want to miss out on ____(1. NAME)____ and ____(2. NAME)____ ! This ____(3. ADJECTIVE)____ young pair of ____(4. COLOR)____ kittens might seem a bit mischievious when they're running off with your ____(5. OBJECT)____ or knocking over your ____(6. OBJECT)____ , but the truth is that they're both sweeter than ____(7. DESSERT)____ . These two aren't just littermates—they're best friends who love to ____(8. VERB)____ , ____(9. VERB)____ , and ____(10. VERB)____ together. They'll crack you up as they ____(11. VERB)____ down the hall, and at the end of the day, they'll fall asleep on your ____(12. FURNITURE)____ while purring louder than a ____(13. TYPE OF VEHICLE)____ . If you're looking for a bonded pair of ____(14. ADJECTIVE)____ kittens, look no further!

NOW THAT YOU'VE FILLED OUT THEIR BIOS, WHICH OF THE CATS WOULD YOU BE MOST INTERESTED IN ADOPTING?

BONDED PAIRS
STICK TOGETHER

When two cats are best friends who love to cuddle and play together, they're called a bonded pair, and it's important for them to stay with each other for life! When duos enter an animal shelter, the adoption team will try to find a home that can adopt both cats so that they can continue to be best friends forever.

CONNECT THE BONDED PAIRS

Four pairs of cats entered the shelter together, and it's your job to figure out a way to keep them together. Draw a series of lines that connect each of the bonded pairs. The lines can't intersect and must be vertical or horizontal (no diagonal lines allowed). Only one line can occupy each grid. Can you solve the problem and keep every bonded pair together?

EXAMPLE:

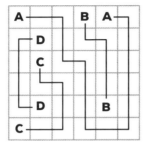

See answers on page 117.

 BELLA and LUNA   SNOWBALL and RAINDROP

 FLUFFY and PUFFY   MAC and CHEESE

SPEAK UP FOR CATS!

One way to be an **ADVOCAT** is by creating short, catchy phrases called slogans. With a bit of hand-lettering, these slogans can be made into T-shirts, educational stickers, or even a poster for your wall. These items can then be used in fundraisers for your local shelter!

HOW TO DRAW A BANNER

SUPPLIES NEEDED:

Paper   Pencil with an eraser

Two markers:
One thick
One thin

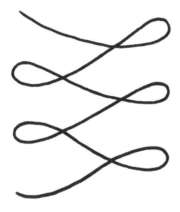

Step 1: Lightly draw a zigzag squiggle with 5 loops with your pencil. Draw this same squiggle a few times and pick out the one you like best.

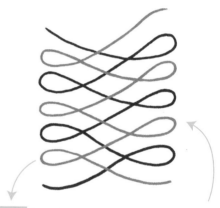

Step 2: Then draw the same 5-looped squiggle in the opoosite direction with your pencil. Begin this squiggle so that the loops will fit in between the lines you've previously drawn.

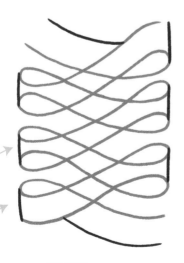

Step 3: Use your pencil to connect your squiggles and make a banner. This part may take some practice, so don't be afraid to try these steps a few times until you get it right. Connect the outside edges of the loops first, then trace along your pencil lines to create each section of banner. Use the top and bottom of your squiggle to create the forked ribbon edges of your banner.

Step 4: Now we're going to fill in the banner with our slogan: "ADOPT DON'T SHOP." Begin by drawing in the edges of the letter first with your thick marker. You can lightly write in each word with pencil first to help you identify where the thick edge of the letter will be.

PRO TIP: Count the number of letters in each word and divide that in half. The letter in the middle will be at the exact center of your banner. Draw that letter in first, then you can draw in the rest of the word around that center letter for an evenly spaced word!

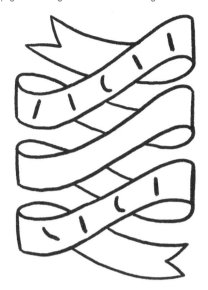

Step 5: Use your thin marker to draw in the rest of each letter.

PRO TIP: The central word "DON'T" is in a blocky font that consists of 4 letters. Lightly draw 4 boxes in that section of banner with a pencil first. Then fill in each box with the letters of the word.

Step 6: Add in fun details like flowers or paw prints. Draw them in lightly with your pencil. Erase the ones you don't like until you get a composition you prefer.

Step 7: Ink over your banner and detail lines using your thick marker. After the marker is completely dry, gently erase all the remaining pencil marks.

NEUTER IS CUTER

🐾 Add a drop-shadow to emphasize a word. Make sure the shadow is always going in the same direction. For example, this shadow is going down and to the right.

🐾 Draw a silhouette shape and fill the shape with your slogan.

SAVE·A·PAW

DON'T DeCLAW!

🐾 Experiment with different fonts and cases. In this composition, upper- and lowercase letters in the same word make it more playful.

it's HIP to be TIPPeD

🐾 Use thick and thin fonts to put emphasis on certain words.

FOSTERING Saves Lives

Use a curved ruler (or use a round object like a bowl or a lid) to help create wavy lines in a composition.

Create small versions of composition ideas first to determine a layout you like. These sketches are called "thumbnails."

Come up with some cat advocacy slogans of your own:

_____

_____

_____

_____

Create some "thumbnail" sketches in the T-shirts below using your new slogans. Pick out your favorite sketch and design your very own cat advocacy shirt on a blank piece of paper!

CAT FURRTOGRAPHY CHALLENGE!

DO YOU HAVE THE PHOTOGRAPHY SKILLS OF A PROFESSIONAL PAWPURRAZZO? OR IS YOUR PHOTO REEL NOTHING BUT BLURRY BLOBS OF FUR?

Volunteering as a photographer is a great way to help adoptable cats find homes by showcasing their personalities up close and personal. A beautiful photo can be included in an adoption profile. It makes a big difference in the likelihood of attracting a forever family!

Cat photography is a skill set that anyone can learn, and once you know a few tricks, you can take fantastic, flattering photos of felines. Whether you're using a digital camera or a smartphone, you can vastly improve your shots by implementing three simple tips:

1. LET THERE BE LIGHT

Using a natural light source, like sunshine coming through a window, will help you get a crisp photo with lots of details. Turn off your flash, open your curtains, and let the sun shine in.

2. GET ON THEIR LEVEL

Hold the lens at eye level with the cat. Looking at a cat head-on helps to create a greater feeling of connection for the viewer.

3. USE TOYS, MAKE NOISE

Tempting items like crinkle balls, jingle balls, and wand toys can be great at capturing a cat's attention. Move the toy just above the camera lens, and they'll look right at you. Then...click! You've got your photo!

PRACTICE YOUR PHOTOGRAPHY SKILLS AT HOME WITH YOUR CAT! SEE HOW MANY OF THESE PHOTO CHALLENGES YOU CAN SUCCESSFULLY COMPLETE.

☐ Looking out the window

☐ Mid-jump

☐ Making a silly face

☐ Tongue sticking out

☐ Asleep

☐ Eating

☐ Playing with a toy

☐ Close-up of face

Close-up of paws ☐

Meowing ☐

Mid-yawn ☐

Headshot ☐

Full body ☐

☐ Close-up of eyes

☐ Drinking water

☐ Posing with a fun prop

☐ Rolling over

☐ About to pounce

☐ In direct sunlight

14 CAREERS FOR CAT PEOPLE

If you want to take your love for cats to the next level, you could consider a career in feline welfare. Here are 14 different job opportunities where you can help make the world a better place for cats.

INSTRUCTIONS: Unscramble the words to discover the feline welfare job titles. Then use the letters in the highlighted boxes to create a motivational phrase!

TAC YTO KRAME ☐☐☐ ☐☐▨ ☐☐☐☐☐

NAILAM LORTCON FICEFOR ☐☐☐☐☐☐ ☐▨☐☐☐☐☐ ☐☐☐☐☐☐☐

NOTIDOPA SEOULCRON ☐☐☐☐☐☐☐☐ ☐☐▨☐☐☐☐☐

CTA FACE FSATF ☐☐☐ ▨☐☐☐☐ ☐☐☐☐☐

TCA ROTHISABVIE ☐☐☐☐ ☐☐☐☐▨☐☐☐☐☐

RATERIVENY CHINETINAC ☐☐☐☐☐☐☐☐☐☐ ☐☐☐☐☐☐☐☐☐▨

MANILA GETAHORPHORP ☐☐☐☐☐☐ ☐☐▨☐☐☐☐☐☐☐

DAVACCOY PIGCAMAN GERMANA ☐☐☐☐☐☐☐☐ ☐☐☐☐☐☐☐☐ ☐☐☐☐☐▨

COTIA DULIBER ☐☐☐☐☐☐ ☐☐☐▨☐☐

TEP RITEST ▨☐☐☐ ☐☐☐☐☐☐

HENUMA RUDETOCA ☐☐☐☐☐☐ ☐☐☐▨☐☐

TRANG TWERIR ☐☐▨☐☐ ☐☐☐☐☐☐

TANNEREVAIRI ☐☐▨☐☐☐☐☐☐☐☐

LAMINA TERELSH EVRAGRICE ☐☐☐☐☐☐ ▨☐☐☐☐☐☐ ☐☐☐☐☐☐☐☐☐

☐☐ ☐☐☐ ☐☐☐☐☐☐☐☐ !

See answers on page 117.

YOU CAN HELP CATS

Each and every one of us has a special way that we can help make a difference for cats. Just about every skill, resource, and interest you have can be used to help our feline friends.

- Are you a baker who likes to make elaborate cakes? Auction off an epic cat cake and give the proceeds to your local rescue.

- Do you have a car? Offer to transport cats for TNR.

- Are you a skater with event-planning skills? Hold a skate-a-thon and have participants pledge a donation for the cats.

- Do you have a special skill, like graphic design or accounting? Reach out and offer to help a local shelter.

Write out a list of the skills, hobbies, interests, and resources you have:

Write three ideas for how you could use your unique abilities to help cats:

1.

2.

3.

INTENTION-SETTING WORKSHEET

THREE ENRICHMENT ACTIVITIES I'D LIKE TO TRY WITH MY CAT:

1.

2.

3.

TWO WAYS I CAN COMMIT TO GIVING MY CAT A HEALTHIER LIFE:

1.

2.

ONE WAY I WANT TO HELP CATS IN SHELTERS THIS YEAR:

SOMETHING I CAN DO TO HELP OUT DURING KITTEN SEASON:

ONE THING I CAN DO TO HELP THE CATS LIVING IN MY COMMUNITY:

SOMETHING I'D LIKE TO EDUCATE MY FRIENDS AND FAMILY ABOUT:

ANSWER KEY

"GROW YOUR OWN CAT GRASS," P. 38
Lilies and azaleas are not cat safe.

"A TRIP TO THE VET," P. 49
WORD BANK

prescription	ear mites	ointment
FVRCP	records	rabies
annual	technician	ringworm
exercise	dental	insurance
fleas	spay	neuter
microchip	dewormer	UTI
antibiotic	fever	stethoscope
clinic	veterinarian	

**"WHAT'S THE SCOOP ON PEE AND POOP?,"
P. 54–55**

1. C
2. D
3. A
4. C
5. D
6. C
7. B
8. D
9. B
10. D

"SAVE THE DAY: NEUTER AND SPAY," P. 56–57

1. 8
2. 32
3. 40
4. 100
5. $8,000
6. $640
7. $160
8. 58
9. 0

"COMMUNITY CAT SEEK & FIND," P. 66–67
How many community cats can you find? 28
How many of the cats have eartips? 12
How many of the cats still need to be spayed or neutered? 16

"ARE YOU MY MOM?," P. 76–77
E. Cats A, C, D, and G all have eartips, which means they've been spayed or neutered. Cats B and F are male. Cat E has visible teats, which means she is lactating—so she must be the mama!

"KITTEN MILESTONE TIMELINE," P. 82–83
Adopted!

"WHAT'S THE WEIGHT?," P. 84–85
1. Beep

2. Meep
3. Bartholomew
4. Meep
5. Angela and Meep
6. Doodle

"THE ROAD TO ADOPTION," P. 100

1. Born in an alley
2. Fed by a local caregiver
3. Taken in temporarily by a neighbor
4. Surrendered to an animal control officer
5. Brought to intake at an animal shelter
6. Taken to the veterinarian
7. Housed in cat room at the shelter
8. Placed in a foster home
9. Brought to an adoption event
10. Adopted into a loving forever home!

"CONNECT THE BONDED PAIRS," P. 105

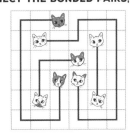

"14 CAREERS FOR CAT PEOPLE," P. 112
Cat Toy Maker
Animal Control Officer
Adoption Counselor
Cat Cafe Staff
Cat Behaviorist
Veterinary Technician
Animal Photographer
Advocacy Campaign Manager
Catio Builder
Pet Sitter
Humane Educator
Grant Writer
Veterinarian
Animal Shelter Caregiver

Motivational phrase: You can help cats!